He Restores My Soul

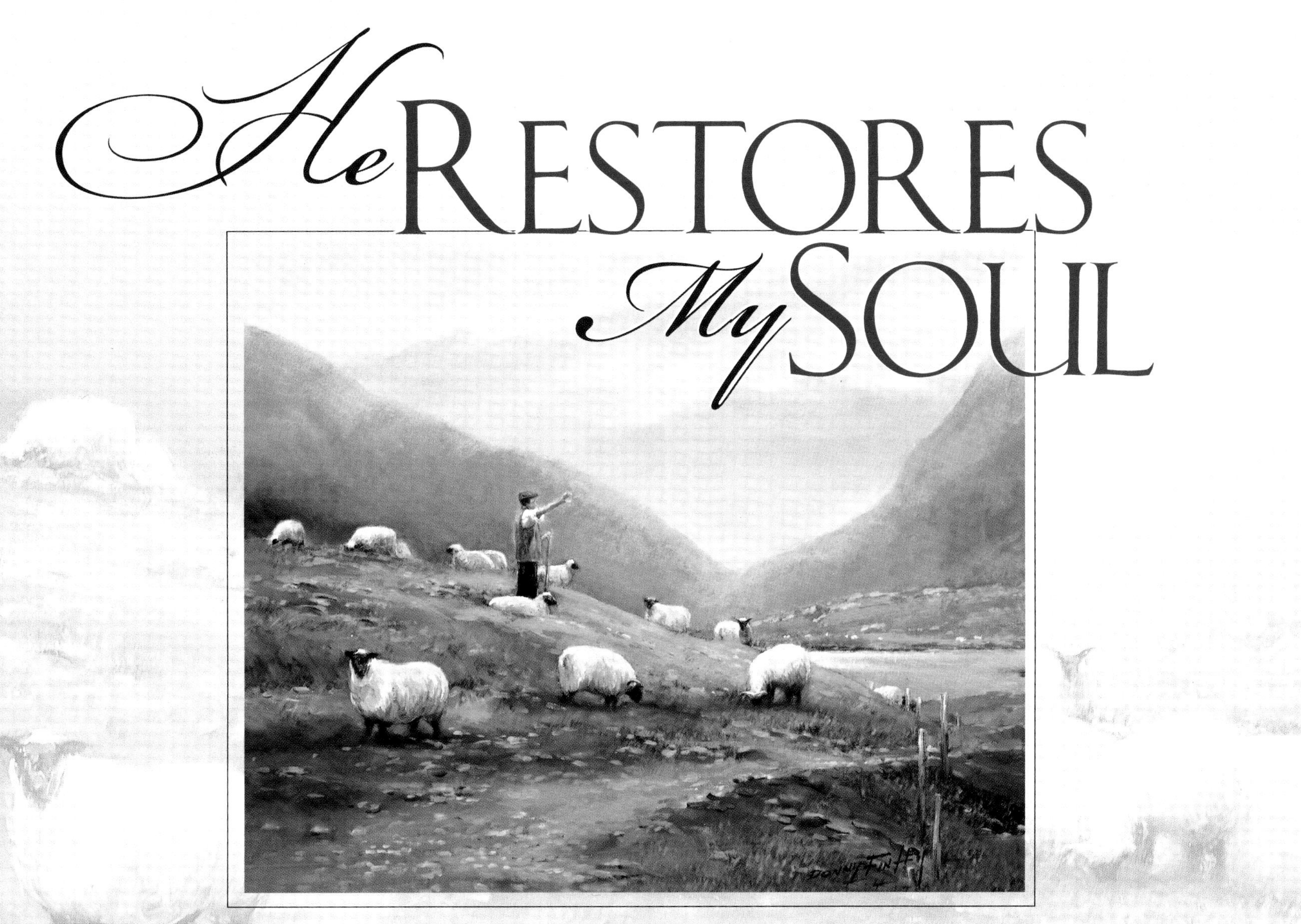

by Donny Finley

Harvest House Publishers
EUGENE, OREGON

He Restores My Soul

Published by Harvest House Publishers
Eugene, Oregon 97402

Library of Congress Cataloging-in Publication Data

Finley, Donny.
He restores my soul/Donny Finley.
p. cm.
ISBN 0-7369-0311-9
1.God—Love—Meditations. 2.Bible. O.T. Psalms XXIII—Meditations. 3 Finley, Donny—Religion. I.Title

BT140 .F56 2000
242´.5—dc2 00-035063

Arts Uniq'
P.O. Box 3085
Cookeville, TN 38502
800-223-5020

Design and production by Koechel Peterson & Associates, Minneapolis, Minnesota

Printed in Hong Kong.

00 01 02 03 04 05 06 07 08 09 / NG / 10 9 8 7 6 5 4 3 2 1

He is your keeper. He has kept you hitherto. Do you but hold fast to His dear hand, and He will lead you safely through all things; and, when you cannot stand, He will bear you in His arms.

St. Francis de Sales

Contents

Where God Guides, He Provides

One of the best-loved passages of Scripture begins, "The Lord is my shepherd; I shall not want." Psalm 95:7 declares, "We are the sheep of His hand." Jesus said of Himself, "I am the good shepherd. The good shepherd lays down his life for the sheep" (John 10:11).

I take great comfort in knowing that I am one of His sheep, that He holds me in His hand. When we know Jesus, we are intimate with the very One who restores our souls and who sends goodness and mercy to follow us all the days of our lives. What a beautiful way to live! It doesn't mean we never have difficulty, but I believe allowing God to guide us brings us to better pastures than we could ever find ourselves. He has a good plan for each one of us. His plan for me was to be an artist. I have tried to please Him and let Him lead and care for me as that plan is lived out.

To me, every painting I do is a miracle. It means so much that people want to have my work in their homes. I don't take that lightly. As He's led me down this path, the Lord has also deposited in my heart some important life lessons, and I have been wanting to share those too. So I have combined words with art in this book to hopefully bless and encourage you. As you read, let the Lord use the words to speak to your heart about His loving, gentle shepherding. Let the art remind you of His constant care for you. No one can walk through this life unwounded, but my prayer is that as you walk with Him, your confident declaration will ever be, "I know He loves me. He restores my soul."

The LORD IS MY SHEPHERD; I

God is too wise not to know all about us, and what is really best for us to be and to have. And He is too good not to desire our highest good, and too powerful, desiring, not to effect it.

H.P. LIDDON

SHALL NOT WANT.

He IS MY PROVIDER

"For I know the plans I have for you," declares the LORD, *"plans to prosper you and not to harm you, plans to give you hope and a future."*

JEREMIAH 29:11

Sons are a heritage from the LORD, children a reward from him.

PSALM 123:3

I can't remember a time when I didn't love the feel of a pencil in my hand. When I was five years old, I often went to visit Charlotte Williams, our kind next-door neighbor. She liked to draw and would invite me to draw with her. If you had asked me then what I wanted to be when I grew up, I would have said an artist.

BEGINNINGS

Besides afternoons with Charlotte, I also had fun at home with the Sears catalogue. I would practice drawing the many wonderful things and people I discovered within its glossy pages. My ever-patient grandmother would look at my pictures and then tell me stories about her life as a child. I look back now and see that the beginnings of my interest in art were gently encouraged by loving adults who thought a young boy's scribbling was worth paying attention to.

He paints the
lily of the field,
Perfumes each lily bell;
If He so loves
the little flowers,
I know He loves
me well.

MARIA STRAUS

The King of Love my Shepherd is,
Whose goodness faileth never,
I nothing lack if I am His,
And He is mine forever.

SIR HENRY WILLIAMS BAKER

FAMILY

When I was growing up, my mom and dad both had to work hard to make a living, so my sister, Patsy, and I spent a lot of time with our grandparents. I wouldn't trade those times together for anything. Those two dear people cared for us with such love. Momma, my grandmother, was a great listener and always good for a story on wet, windy days. Pappa and I often poked around outside together. Among other things, he taught me the joys of fishing and hunting—and of simply loving life.

Though my dad worked long hours, every now and then we would sneak off together to shoot pool; afterward we'd get hamburgers. Also, when he had time on the weekends, *both* he and my grandfather would take me fishing. A boy can't get a better deal than that.

I smiled at Grandpa. Grandpa's my best friend.

Patricia Hermes
A Place for Jeremy

Overflowing Abundance

How priceless is your unfailing love! Both high and low among men find refuge in the shadow of your wings. They feast on the abundance of your house; you give them drink from your river of delights.

PSALM 36:7,8

Your bounty is beyond my speaking, but though my mouth be dumb, my heart shall thank You.

NICHOLAS ROWE

Our God is such a generous provider. The book of Luke tells the story of Simon Peter fishing all night and coming up with nothing (Luke 5:5-7). But when Jesus got in his boat, He told Simon to go out to the deep water and let down the net for a catch. And Simon said, "'Master, we've worked hard all night and haven't caught anything. But because you say so, I will let down the nets.' When they had done so, they caught such a large number of fish that their nets began to break. So they signaled their partners in the other boats to come and help them, and they came and filled both boats so full that they began to sink." Peter's response is so much like mine. I'll work—and work *hard*—and nothing comes. Then the Lord will ask me to go further out and my response is often, "I've done all that and it hasn't worked, and now I'm supposed to go out further? I'm supposed to try this and be just a little more risky? I think I need to stay here where it's safe." Jesus simply asked Peter to go out into the deep water and let down his nets for a catch. And like Peter, when I have honored Him with my obedience, He has never failed to provide me with overflowing abundance.

Moment by moment
I'm kept in His love,
Moment by moment
I've life from above;
Looking to Jesus
till glory doth shine,
Moment by moment,
O Lord, I am Thine.

MAJOR DANIEL WEBSTER WHITTLE

God proves that He is a provider in the most amazing ways. Where no fish were, suddenly there are enough to break the nets. Out of nothing He created the world and everything in it. I love painting images of His creation and capturing the beauty He has so bountifully placed on the earth. From small beginnings He led me to become a painter.

I grew up in a very small community, and the nearest thing we had to art was an encyclopedia that had pictures of paintings in it. Yet one incredible, unforgettable day when I was in the fifth grade, I found a picture called "Albert's Son" by Andrew Wyeth. It touched me, and God used it to speak to my heart about the gift He had placed in my life. I didn't have to wander through famous museums filled with incredible art to find that painting…I simply opened the pages of a book and found it there.

BLESSINGS

Nor need we power or splendor, wide hall or lordly dome;

The good, the true, the tender—these form the wealth of home.

SARAH J. HALE

I was blessed with the best Mom and Dad in the world. They supported me in so many ways—I wouldn't be an artist now if it weren't for them. When I first started displaying my art, I would sometimes have to paint until after midnight. Then we'd all get up at the crack of dawn so we could be at the show early in the morning. My parents would willingly stay up late, cutting mats and making frames, sometimes right up to the last minute. In those days, that was a major part of my life. My mother and grandmother took my paintings to shows on the weekends when I was in college. Those sweet ladies sold my artwork so that I could go to school. All through my life, my parents and grandparents have been there for me, demonstrating their unconditional support by countless acts of sacrificial love.

Psalm 23:1 reminds me that I can live a life without want. My family wasn't rich in material possessions, but in the things of life that count, we were very rich indeed.

I have my own family now—a wonderful wife and three beautiful daughters. My prayer for my girls has always been that they will follow in their father's footsteps...not necessarily as an artist, but as a person who loves the Lord with all his heart and looks to Him to be the source of his every need.

O Christ, in Thee my soul hath found,
And found in Thee alone,
The peace, the joy I sought so long,
The bliss till now unknown.

I sighed for rest and happiness,
I yearned for them, not Thee;
But while I passed my Saviour by,
His love laid hold on me.

Now none but Christ can satisfy,
None other name for me;
There's love, and life, and lasting joy,
Lord Jesus, found in Thee.

AUTHOR UNKNOWN

He MAKES ME TO LIE DOWN IN

He LEADS ME BESIDE THE

He brought his people out like a flock; he led them like sheep through the desert.

He guided them safely, so they were unafraid.

PSALM 78:52,53

GREEN PASTURES STILL WATERS

He IS MY GUIDE

Like a river glorious is God's perfect peace,
Over all victorious in its bright increase;
Perfect, yet it floweth fuller every day,
Perfect, yet it groweth deeper all the way.
Stayed upon Jehovah, hearts are fully blest;
Finding, as He promised, perfect peace and rest.

FRANCES RIDLEY HAVERGAL

I will place over them one shepherd, my servant David, and he will tend them; he will tend them and be their shepherd.

EZEKIEL 34:23

Even after David had become king, he did not forget what it was to care for sheep—long years of dwelling in pastureland had shaped his shepherd's heart. One day as he sat upon his lofty throne he remembered his friend and asked, "Is there anyone still left of the house of Saul to whom I can show kindness for Jonathan's sake?" (2 Samuel 9:1). And like a little, crippled sheep, Jonathan's son Mephibosheth was discovered in hiding, afraid for his life. But David sought him out, acknowledged who he was, and restored to him his inheritance. Our Shepherd over and over shows us this same compassion. Though we are God's children, the people of His pasture and the sheep of His hand, we may be hiding because of fear or sin. However, He does not lose sight of us—He finds us out, identifies us, and gives us the promise of a glorious inheritance waiting in heaven that is also realized in part in our daily walk with Him.

O come, let us worship and bow down: let us kneel before the Lord our maker. For he is our God; and we are the people of his pasture, and the sheep of his hand.

PSALM 95:6,7 (KJV)

"We Are the People of His Pasture . . ."

Still Waters

Though I was very loved and cared for as a child, occasionally I experienced feelings of fear. Even as an adult, I have to admit that every now and then I lie awake at night. Running a gallery, putting children through school, providing for a family, and the struggle I go through creating a painting sometimes seems as if they are more than I can handle. But then I remember that God has provided His Word and presence to comfort and strengthen me. "For He Himself has said, 'I will never leave you nor forsake you.' So we may boldly say: 'The Lord is my helper; I will not fear'" (Hebrews 13:5,6 NKJ). The next time you are anxious, do not fear, but look to the Lord who is your helper. Wherever you are, whatever your circumstances, He can guide you to green pastures and lead you beside still waters.

I will lie down and sleep in peace, for you alone, O LORD, make me dwell in safety.

PSALM 4:8

Where streams of living water flow
My ransomed soul He leadeth,
And where the verdant pastures grow,
With food celestial feedeth.

Sir Henry Williams Baker

You have hedged me behind and before,
and laid Your hand upon me.

PSALM 139:5 (NKJ)

He Promises Peace

I wish I could say I always know the way to go, but I have to admit that sometimes I don't. Yet I do know the hand of the Lord is always upon me. When the way before me is a little dark, I can turn to His Word, which is "a lamp to my feet and a light for my path" (Psalm 119:105). I can relax, knowing that "the steps of a good man are ordered by the LORD, and He delights in his way" (Psalm 37:23, NKJ). As I move forward in everyday activities, I can trust that He has ordered those things for me. I let His peace lead me. "I will listen to what God the LORD will say; he promises peace to his people" (Psalm 85:8).

I believe in God, in the same way in which I believe in my friends, because I feel the breath of His love and His invisible, intangible hand, bringing me here, carrying me there, pressing upon me.

MIGUEL DE UNAMUNO

The Shadow of the Almighty

The Lord watches over you—the Lord is your shade at your right hand.

Psalm 121:5

I recently completed a picture for my church. From the beginning, I wanted it to be a simple shepherd scene. As I painted, the Lord reminded me of the beautiful words of Psalm 91, "He who dwells in the shelter of the Most High will rest in the shadow of the Almighty." Sometimes I find myself overwhelmed with all I have to get done: commission paintings, this book, a show out of town. Those are the times I need to pause and remember, with all that's going on, that I am able to rest in His shadow. He provides shade just when I need it.

Psalm 23:2 reminds me I can trust Jesus to show me the way to blessings. "He leads me beside the still waters." I don't know what is ahead in my future, but I do know how I will get there. I will be closely following my Shepherd.

Go out into the darkness and put your hand into the Hand of God. That shall be to you better than light and safer than a known way.

Minnie Louise Haskins

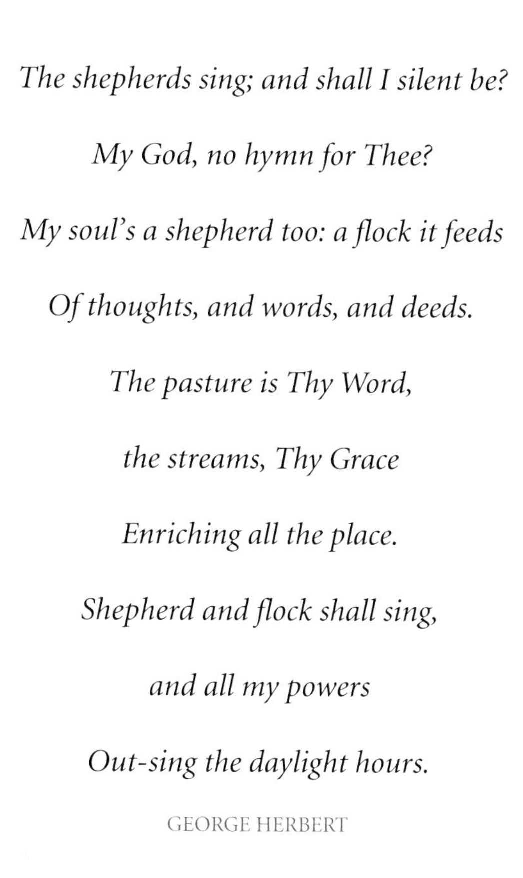

The shepherds sing; and shall I silent be?

My God, no hymn for Thee?

My soul's a shepherd too: a flock it feeds

Of thoughts, and words, and deeds.

The pasture is Thy Word,

the streams, Thy Grace

Enriching all the place.

Shepherd and flock shall sing,

and all my powers

Out-sing the daylight hours.

GEORGE HERBERT

PSALM 91

He who dwells in the shelter of the Most High will rest in the shadow of the Almighty.

I will say of the Lord, "He is my refuge and my fortress, my God, in whom I trust."

Surely he will save you from the fowler's snare and from the deadly pestilence. He will cover you with his feathers, and under his wings you will find refuge; his faithfulness will be your shield and rampart.

You will not fear the terror of night, nor the arrow that flies by day, nor the pestilence that stalks in the darkness, nor the plague that destroys at midday.

A thousand may fall at your side, ten thousand at your right hand, but it will not come near you.

You will only observe with your eyes and see the punishment of the wicked. If you make the Most High your dwelling—even the Lord, who is my refuge—then no harm will befall you, no disaster will come near your tent.

For he will command his angels concerning you to guard you in all your ways; they will lift you up in their hands, so that you will not strike your foot against a stone.

You will tread upon the lion and the cobra; you will trample the great lion and the serpent.

"Because he loves me," says the Lord, "I will rescue him; I will protect him, for he acknowledges my name.

"He will call upon me, and I will answer him; I will be with him in trouble, I will deliver him and honor him.

"With long life will I satisfy him and show him my salvation."

UNDER HIS WINGS

The LORD is near to all who call on him.

PSALM 145:18

Satisfy us in the morning with your unfailing love, that we may sing for joy and be glad all our days.

PSALM 90:14

Because God is my hiding place, I am learning I need no other place of safety. "I will say of the LORD, He is my refuge and my fortress, my God in whom I trust" (Psalm 91:2). I love this imagery. Though I am glad for the strength of the fortress, I am also grateful for the security chicks feel when cuddled in the warmth and closeness of their mother's wings.

My wife, Janet, and I often pray Psalm 91 over our children. As they grow and learn to adjust to school, peer pressure, and other difficult life issues, we proclaim: "God will cover you with His feathers and under His wings you will find refuge; His faithfulness will be your shield and your rampart." We rest easier as parents knowing we can entrust our little chicks to His daily care and keeping.

For my own life, when I treasure these words in my heart, I find peace for the task and help for the journey: "If you make the Most High your dwelling—even the LORD, who is my refuge—then no harm will befall you...for he will command his angels concerning you to guard you in all your ways..." (Psalm 91:5-11). "Because he loves me," says the LORD, "I will rescue him; I will protect him, for he acknowledges my name. He will call upon me, and I will answer him; I will be with him in trouble, I will deliver him and honor him. With long life will I satisfy him, and show him my salvation" (verses 14-16).

He restores my soul; He leads ... of righteousness for His

For thus says the Lord God, Behold, I Myself will search for My sheep and seek them out. As a shepherd cares for his herd…so I will care for My sheep.

Ezekiel 34:11,12 (NASB)

ME IN THE PATHS
NAME'S SAKE.

He IS MY SAVIOR

We never know where God hides His pools. We see a rock, and we cannot guess it is the home of the spring. We see a flinty place, and we cannot tell it is the hiding place of a fountain. God leads me into the hard places, and then I find I have gone into the dwelling place of eternal springs.

AUTHOR UNKNOWN

He leadeth me, O blessed thought! O words with heavenly comfort fraught! Whate'er I do, where'er I be—still 'tis God's hand that leadeth me.

Joseph Henry Gilmore

Though I grew up in a Christian home, and Patsy and I sang in churches all over our community, I didn't accept Christ as my Savior until I was 12 years old. Yet, even then, He wasn't the one who ruled my heart. I was deep in the Savior, but He was never really the Lord. But God never gave up on me, even though by the time I got to college I had drifted from His side. He never stopped wanting to lead me in paths of righteousness. I began to feel His gentle nudging about the way I was living my life, so I prayed for a wife who would be a good influence on me. After Janet and I were married, we started attending church and home meetings, and my walk with the Lord began to increase in depth and strength. I discovered that I had only been leaning on Him when I felt a need for Him, and He was yearning for a deeper relationship with me. Now I can say He is Friend, Brother, and Father. He's truly everything.

Truly Everything

LIGHT

One of the greatest ways my Christian life influences my painting is with the image of light—I try to weave in as much as I can. In a dream one night, I saw God's Word open before me and it was glowing. It was like light magnified.

Your word is a lamp to my feet and a light for my path.

PSALM 119:105

My favorite imagery of light is the kind that is brilliant, dense in its center, and then grays as it spreads outward. In doorways you can see the light invading the darkness. When we have Jesus and the power of His Word inside us, then we can permeate dark corners of our world with His light.

Once I was in a situation in which I had a deadline to complete a painting. I had been working and working on this piece for a couple of months. This beautiful scene in Italy had an archway with old stone walls. The stones' surface was gray, but when the sun hit it just right, the light that had been soaked up for centuries seemed to emanate from it. I was trying to work from photographs, and though I had the image in my mind, I just couldn't get it onto the canvas. I stayed up all night trying to finish it, but about 4:00 A.M. I was at the end of myself. I finally set the painting against the window and sat down on the couch in front of it and began to pray. "Lord, I've done everything I can do. You've got to help me in some way." I raised my head and looked out the window and saw the first light of the new day coming through the trees. That sunrise hit the back of the mesh canvas. The painting began to glow from within. Everywhere I needed to paint light was lit from the rays of God's sun. I had that impossible painting finished in literally 45 minutes.

Sometimes I just don't know how to do the things I know I am called to do. But I have this assurance: As I begin each day with prayer, He lights up my life. He restores my soul.

When God and His glory are made our end, we shall find a silent likeness pass in upon us; the beauty of God will, by degrees, enter upon our soul.

STEPHEN CHARNOCK

Oh, the pure delight of a single hour that before the throne I spend,
When I kneel in prayer and with Thee Oh God,
I commune as friend with Friend.

FANNY CROSBY

The wonderful message of salvation is the best news the world has ever received. When I was a child, I thought salvation was only about getting to heaven. But knowing Jesus as Savior means so much more than that. Our Shepherd truly is concerned about our daily needs and He cares very much about the condition of our souls. Salvation is definitely an eternal thing, but it's also a very present thing.

Don't think so much about who is for or against you, rather give all your care, that God be with you in everything you do.

THOMAS Á KEMPIS

Psalm 23:3 reminds me that "he leads me in the path of righteousness." I look over my life and am amazed at how faithful He has been. In college, I majored in business, not art. But I took a course called "Introduction to Art" that included some art history and drawing. When I was a sophomore, I attended a local outdoor art show, saw that people were selling things, and decided to give it a try. I sold a few paintings at the first show I participated in—at the second show I won first place. I began exhibiting at these shows on a regular basis, and by the time I was a senior I was paying all my school tuition and expenses from the sale of my art. After graduation I decided to give myself a year to make it as an artist, and I have been painting ever since. Every day I see that His hand is on my life and endeavors to provide for my family. He has shown me, after all this time, that I can confidently rest in Him.

Thou art worthy, O Lord,
to receive glory and honor and power:
for thou hast created all things,
and for thy pleasure they are
and were created.

REVELATION 4:11 (KJV)

Know that the LORD is God. It is he who made us, and we are his; we are his people, the sheep of his pasture.

PSALM 100:3

The Wonderful Message

What do you think? If a man owns a hundred sheep, and one of them wanders away, will he not leave the ninety-nine on the hills and go to look for the one that wandered off?

MATTHEW 18:12

The Scarlet Thread

One night as I was lying in bed and thinking about the young shepherd watching over his flock in the painting on this page, God began to speak to me about His constant watching over His sheep. I call this painting "The Scarlet Thread," and it shows us the Shepherd's willingness to leave the 99 who are safe to find the one who is lost. I am so glad He found me. Let me share with you a few of the images from this painting He used to deeply touch my life.

He showed me that the purple shawl Jesus wears symbolizes His royalty; we serve the King of kings and Lord of lords! Jesus is also wearing a scarlet cord around His waist, representing the blood He shed for us that makes it possible to have an intimate, life-changing relationship with Him. I have noticed a scarlet thread of redemption running all through the Bible, from the Passover lamb to Rahab's salvation during the destruction of Jericho, and culminating with Jesus' death on the cross. He was the perfect sacrifice that frees us forever from that which separates us from a holy God.

Other images in this painting are precious to me. The stripes on the boy's shirt represent the stripes Jesus bore that I might be healed. Jesus' presence in the field proclaims the message that He did not stay buried in a tomb, but rose from the grave to live each day with me. Jesus is also carrying a lamb—one He left the 99 for to rescue and bring back to the safety of the field. And the bucket the little shepherd carries reminds me that my own life is a container for the Holy Spirit, who is my Helper and Comforter.

I know that David, once a worshipful shepherd, was also a man after God's own heart. I want to be that kind of man too. In the dark of night, when I think about what Jesus has done for me, I find my heart yearns a little more closely after Him.

Yea THOUGH I WALK THROUGH THE VALLEY OF THE SHADOW OF DEATH, I WILL FEAR NO EVIL; FOR YOU ARE WITH ME; YOUR ROD AND YOUR STAFF, THEY COMFORT ME.

He Gives Me Comfort

God has been gracious to me and I have all I need.

GENESIS 33:11

Each of us may be sure that if God sends us on stony paths He will provide us with strong shoes, and He will not send us out on any journey for which He does not equip us well.

MACLAREN

adow of death
esence, which
with comfort.
One day I was
n I was under
onth, and the
d to pray with
erson at home
to involve her
nd we prayed
l voice coming
r more clearly,
int well." I was

atie, Leah, and

Before they call I will answer; while they are still speaking I will hear.

ISAIAH 65:24

God does not basically give grace because there is a need, but God gives grace because He is a gracious God.

Johnny Foglander

Loving influences…they blow into our lives like a gentle breeze to soothe and calm our spirits. God has placed some wonderful people in my life who represent His tender care. These are the people He often sends to walk beside me when I am in the valley. Though His presence never leaves me, I also have the joy of fellowship with people I have come to trust and love.

Great is my confidence in you…I am filled with comfort.

2 CORINTHIANS 7:4 (NASB)

My pastor, Raymond Culpepper, has always been a source of grace and guidance for me. When I'm going through something that's really tough, I always run into Joe Medina. I can talk anything over with him. My friend Steve Sampson is different. Though his wit is dry, all of a sudden his insightful point can hit me like a sledgehammer. Isa Bajalia is on the mission field in Israel, where I know he prays for me faithfully. Brother Carl Delatte calls from the mission field just to talk about what God is doing in our lives.

But undoubtedly, the most important person in my life is Janet. The great thing about our marriage is that when I'm at the bottom of the heap, she is strong. When she's down, I am strong. We make a perfect team.

God wants to comfort you and to protect you from evil even in the valley of the shadow of death. Sometimes it isn't physical death we are dealing with. The shadow can hover over a dream, a hope, a prayer. Like a sheep, stick close to your Shepherd. There is no need to fear when you walk with Him.

LOVING

INFLUENCES

An infinite God can give all of Himself to each of His children. He does not distribute Himself that each may have a part, but to each one He gives all of Himself as fully as if there were no others.

A.W. TOZER

SAVING GRACE

One of the stories my grandmother used to tell me was about how God had saved her life. After my grandfather came to know the Lord, he wanted so badly to have a meeting in his home. Their preacher back then was a man who simply traveled from place to place. The day finally came, and my grandparents were getting ready and trying to ignore the ominous weather. My grandfather was helping people get in from the rain, my grandmother was sweeping up at the doorway, and my mother, just a small child, was busy playing at my grandmother's feet. Just as the preacher began speaking, a tornado struck.

My grandmother remembered picking up my mother before blacking out. She awoke in a field, my mother still tight in her arms, several hundred yards away from where the house had stood. Miraculously, both of them were virtually unharmed. If my mother had died in that tornado, I wouldn't be here. I am so grateful her brief moments in the valley of the shadow of death were covered by God's hand.

He mounted the cherubim and flew; he soared on the wings of the wind...the LORD was my support. He brought me out into a spacious place...because he delighted in me.

2 SAMUEL 22:11,20

Though winds are wild, and the gale unleashed,

My trusting heart still sings:

I know that they mean no harm to me,

He rideth on their wings.

AUTHOR UNKNOWN

STILL TRUSTING

Your heavenly Father is too good to be unkind and too wise to make mistakes.

CHARLES H. SPURGEON

Trust in Him at all times, O people; pour out your heart before Him; God is a refuge for us.

PSALM 62:8 (NASB)

Yet, it is sometimes hard when the saving doesn't seem to be there. It hurts to watch my father, who had always been such a rock for me, struggle now with Alzheimer's and cancer. But I continue to believe God is in complete control. I don't understand everything, but because I have experienced over and over again His marvelous grace, I am convinced of His goodness and love.

GOD *is* BIGGER

One of my favorite stories in the Bible is about the woman who presses through the crowd to Jesus (Luke 8:43-48). This woman's persistence reminds me that every now and then, when I need a touch from the Lord, I need to be pressing through the crowded things on my schedule to get close enough to Him to make a difference. His healing power is there for me as I choose to reach out for it. And He always acknowledges the effort.

Daughter, your faith has healed you. Go in peace.

LUKE 8:48

And the woman wasn't the only person in need. Jairus, a ruler of the synagogue, had also come to Jesus. In fact, Jesus was on his way to Jairus' house to heal his small daughter. But before they could get there, she died. When Jesus and Jairus did arrive, everyone around was screaming and wailing about the little girl being dead. You can imagine how Jairus felt. But Jesus said, "Don't be afraid; just believe, and she will be healed" (Luke 8:50). Jesus was able to make a difference. He brought life back to her. He can do the same with us. With the Lord, it is never too late.

Behold, You desire truth in the inward parts, and in the hidden part You will make me to know wisdom.

PSALM 51:6 (NKJ)

I am the good shepherd; I know my sheep and my sheep know me—just as the Father knows me and I know the Father—and I lay down my life for the sheep.

JOHN 10:14,15

When everybody around us sees no hope, we have to choose to believe and rest in God's Word. It doesn't matter if everybody else is saying, "Well, the child is already dead." It doesn't matter if everybody else is saying, "It's no use. You're going to fail." It doesn't matter if everybody else is saying, "You've lost everything." We must believe that God is bigger than the most awful circumstances and choose to say, "I will fear no evil, for You are with me."

In perplexities—when we cannot tell what to do, when we cannot understand what is going on around us—let us be calmed and steadied and made patient by the thought that what is hidden from us is not hidden from Him.

FRANCES RIDLEY HAVERGAL

Psalm 23:4 reminds me that I do not walk alone in sunshine or in shade. I don't have to understand everything in my life as long as I understand that He is utterly trustworthy. He is bigger than any situation I face.

As one whom his mother comforts, so I will comfort you.

ISAIAH 66:13 (NASB)

He Careth for You

Cast all your care upon Jesus,
Who ever careth for you,
He will sustain and uphold you,
He will be faithful and true.

Jesus, our blessed Redeemer,
Jesus, our Shepherd and Guide,
Ever will bear all your burdens,
Ever will stay by your side.

Jesus knows all of your problems,
Knows all our trial and care,
He's ever ready to help us,
Ready to answer our prayer.

Oh! what a comfort in trial,
Just to lean hard on this Friend,
Trust Him for grace and deliverance,
Learning on Him to depend.

Jesus wants you to be happy,
Wants you to have peace and rest;
Cast all your care then upon Him,
Lean on His strong, loving breast.

Careth? Oh yes! Jesus careth,
His own are dear to His heart;
All His beloved whom He died for,
They are to Him set apart.

Oh! how He cares for His people,
Guards them and keeps them alway,
Wants them to share in His glory,
All through eternity's day.

Make your requests then to Jesus,
Trusting His promise so true;
Roll on the Lord all your burden,
For He is caring for you.

Lois Beckwith

He SHOW

You PREPARE A TABLE BEFORE
ME IN THE PRESENCE OF MY ENEMIES;
YOU ANOINT MY HEAD WITH OIL;
MY CUP RUNS OVER.

God doesn't want us to know that He is faithful just because the Bible says so, but He wants to show Himself faithful in our lives.

ROBERT EKH

ERS ME WITH VICTORY

I am still confident of this: I will see the goodness of the LORD in the land of the living. Wait for the LORD; be strong and take heart and wait for the LORD.

PSALM 27:13,14

But because my servant Caleb...follows me wholeheartedly, I will bring him into the land he went to, and his descendants will inherit it.

NUMBERS 14:24

I love the story of Joshua and Caleb—I am always so encouraged by their faith. They were part of the group of men sent to spy out the Promised Land. Ten of the spies came back and said, "'We went into the land to which you sent us, and it does flow with milk and honey! Here is its fruit. But the people who live there are powerful...We seemed like grasshoppers in our own eyes and looked the same to them'" (Numbers 13:27,28,33). But not Joshua and Caleb. They believed they could take the land because their faith in the God who led them was greater than the giants they had just seen.

Though they did not doubt God's ability to make a way for them, they had to wait a while for their inheritance. Finally, after 40 years of wandering in the desert, the children of Israel crossed the Jordan River. Then they had to trust God to give them victory in battle so that they could occupy the land. It was five more years before they rested from war. At that time, when Caleb was offered the choice of his inheritance, he chose the hill country. It was as if he said, "I want the high land. I want higher ground." I have learned that if I want the best that God has for me, if I'm going to take that high land, then I am going to face giants. But because I seek to have the faith of Joshua and Caleb in my heart and life, I know God can make me victorious.

TAKING THE LAND

God never puts any person in a space too small to grow in.

AUTHOR UNKNOWN

For the Lord is good and his love endures forever; his faithfulness continues through all generations.

PSALM 100:5

His ENDURING LOVE

A few quiet moments each morning with Him helps me to be victorious in battle. Everyday I begin my prayer time with praise. "Jehoshaphat appointed men to sing to the LORD and to praise him for the splendor of his holiness as they went out at the head of the army, saying: 'Give thanks to the LORD, for his love endures forever.' As they began to sing and praise, the LORD set ambushes against the men…who were invading Judah, and they were defeated" (2 Chronicles 20:21,22). Making mention of the Lord's enduring love is a powerful thing, and can bring about defeat to the enemy. Thanking Him for His goodness and praising Him for His faithfulness is a great way to start each day and allows us to possess the promised land He has for us.

O beloved, I plead with you not to treat God's promises as something to be displayed in a museum but to use them as everyday sources of comfort. And whenever you have a time of need, trust the Lord.

CHARLES H. SPURGEON

Building a Memorial

One of the most amazing, encouraging stories in the entire Bible is found in the first few chapters of the book of Joshua. After 40 years of wandering in the wilderness, the time has come for Joshua to lead the children of Israel into the Promised Land, and while the Jordan River is quite a barrier, it is not too great for God. At the banks of the Jordan the priests carrying the Ark of the Covenant are commanded to stand in the river. When they do that, the water piles up and stops flowing.

> *When the whole nation had finished crossing the Jordan, the* L*ORD said to Joshua, "Choose twelve men from among the people, one from each tribe, and tell them to take up twelve stones from the middle of the Jordan from right where the priests stood and to carry them over with you and put them down at the place where you stay tonight." So Joshua called together the twelve men he had appointed from the Israelites, one from each tribe, and said to them, "...Each of you is to take up a stone on his shoulder, according to the number of the tribes of the Israelites, to serve as a sign among you" (Joshua 4:1-6).*

Let never day or night
unhallow'd pass,
But still remember what the
Lord hath done.
William Shakespeare

God had leaders of each tribe bring stones from the middle of the river so that they could build a memorial to the miracle of crossing the river. I need to do that too. I find it so important to be able to look back in hard times and recall how He has been faithful in the past. These places of remembrance honor Him and encourage me when I am going through difficult times. Remembering how He parted the waters before helps me know I can trust Him for the next obstacle I face.

A Stone from the Jordan

Thou spread'st a table in my sight;
Thy unction grace bestoweth;
And O what transport of delight
From Thy pure chalice floweth!

SIR HENRY WILLIAMS BAKER

This is a sane, wholesome, practical working faith: That it is a man's business to do the will of God; second, that God himself takes on the care of that man; and third, that therefore that man ought never to be afraid of anything.

GEORGE MACDONALD

I was under contract to a gallery to promote and sell my paintings for a period of eleven years. As I approached the age of forty, I felt the desire to leave the security of the contract and go out on my own. In doing so, I faced many obstacles. However, through all the trials, I was able to see God's direction in my life. It was a trememdous faith-building experience. Not only did Janet and I grow closer as one, but we both had to draw near to God, who would guide us daily.

So many wonderful, new things happened in our lives from making this change. I had always wanted to go to Italy to paint; we finally did that. The first painting I did after we came back was the one with the stone walls and the archway. I remember when I saw the light coming from the early rising sun and lighting that painting from the back, it seemed like an answer from heaven. That moment is one of my memorials to God's light and faithfulness—one of the stones I took from the Jordan.

My Cup Runs Over

After we returned from Italy, we decided to have a really big show. Janet cared for the gallery, and I snatched a few hours of sleep between paintings. I did this for several months in order to have enough pieces ready. Finally the big day arrived. We had planned on opening the show on a Friday night. I had one painting left that was still giving me trouble. I woke up the Thursday before the Friday night opening and still wasn't through with this painting. So I worked all night on it—and didn't finish it. I finally went to bed Friday morning. When I woke up late that afternoon and went down to the gallery, Janet had sold only one painting.

Then it started snowing. Serious snow. We received 18 inches that night. Janet and I were stranded and, of course, nobody came to the show.

He delights in unchanging love.

Micah 7:18 (NASB)

One of our friends put chains on his tires and rescued us. Janet's parents had taken the kids for the evening, so we arrived home alone to an empty, dark house with no power. We had sunk all our resources into getting ready for the show, and we were as discouraged as we have ever been. And that unfinished painting just sat there, reminding us of months of effort that seemed for nothing. Janet said, "What are we going to do?" I didn't know what to tell her. But I knew that God had moved before in our lives, and I was trusting Him to do that again. Suddenly, I was inspired. "I think we should run a small notice in the paper and say we're going to have the show on Sunday afternoon the following week."

That Sunday afternoon about 200 people showed up.

The first painting we sold was the painting I had been struggling to complete. As Janet and I sat in our cold house all that week, I tackled it again—and won. It was a marvelous painting that brought in more than I had believed possible a few days earlier. Over the next two weeks, we sold just about every painting we had. God was so good to us. When it seemed as though it was literally the end, He overcame snow and creative block to bless us with great prosperity.

You prepare a table before me in the presence of my enemies; You anoint my head with oil; my cup runs over…

Psalm 23:5 reminds me that He can lift me above the most disastrous of circumstances. What seemed like the lowest point in my life ended up being a place of great strength for me as I leaned totally on Him. I couldn't believe in myself or in other people—even the weather was out of my control—but I do not serve a little God. He is so utterly reliable for every situation I face. He prepared a table for me in the presence of my enemy, He anointed my head (and paintbrush) with oil, my cup ran over.

So near, so very near to God
Nearer I could not be;
For in the person of His Son,
I am as near as He.

So dear, so very dear to God,
I could not dearer be;
The love wherewith He loves His Son,
Such is His love to me.

AUTHOR UNKNOWN

"A Secret Place"

I love the painting that appears on this page. As with "The Scarlet Thread," its images are full of hope and refuge. That special night when God spoke to me about "The Scarlet Thread," He also spoke to my heart about the painting here, "A Secret Place."

Many of the symbols from "The Scarlet Thread" are present in "A Secret Place," yet, while "The Scarlet Thread" illustrates our being found by the Shepherd when we stray, "A Secret Place" pictures for us what it is to abide in the shadow of the Almighty (Psalm 91). I believe that secret place of safety for us is at the feet of a living Jesus, Son of the living God.

David was probably a young boy, like the one in the painting, when he slew Goliath. How one that is young have faith that is strong enough, high enough, to defeat a giant? He remembered how God had been with him to fight the bear and lion and help him win. When I face giants in my life, I need to remember times past when God was with me and helped me overcome my enemies.

Yet we are not always fighting bears, lions and giants. There are times when we get to sit beside quiet water. The young shepherd in this painting is resting at the feet of Jesus. Next to him is a sweetly bubbling stream, pouring out water for his refreshment and for the sheep. Jesus said, "Whoever drinks the water I give him will not thirst. Indeed, the water I give him will become in him a spring of water welling up to eternal life" (John 4:14).

I want the water welling up in my life, both for me and to give to others. He promises it to those who come to Him for a drink.

SURELY GOODNESS AND MERCY SHALL FOLLOW
MY LIFE, AND I WILL DWELL IN THE HOUSE OF

He PRO

His banner over me is love
THE SONG OF SONGS 2:4

ME ALL THE DAYS OF
THE LORD FOREVER.

MISES ABIDING LOVE

He is my Altar, I His holy place; I am His guest,
and He my living food; I'm His by penitence, He
is mine by grace; I'm His by purchase, He is mine
by blood; He's my supporting elm, and I His vine:
Thus I my Best-beloved's am; thus He is mine.

FRANCIS QUARLES

Let nothing disturb thee,
Let nothing affright thee,
All things are passing,
God changeth never.

HENRY WADSWORTH
LONGFELLOW

Life will be brighter than noonday, and darkness will become like morning. You will be secure, because there is hope; you will look about you and take your rest in safety. You will lie down, with no one to make you afraid, and many will court your favor.

JOB 11:17-19

There is something about death that causes one to be reflective. We are reminded that nothing lasts forever or stays the same. My grandmother died last year and my grandfather has been gone for a long time. My father is struggling with both cancer and Alzheimer's. But as bad as his condition is, I really don't see that when I visit him…I see my mother. My father's health is not easy to deal with, but my mother remains strong and manages to maintain a wonderful sense of humor. Somehow, goodness and mercy follow her. She has strength for her life because the Lord gives her enough for the task. When I think about things being difficult for me, I look at her and her ability to deal with her life. She is an amazing woman. Watching her reminds me of God's grace and unconditional love for each one of us. My mom's love for my dad is about as perfect, as changeless, as I have ever seen.

Everlasting Joy

Isaiah 61 is a beautiful chapter about the Lord's kindness and favor. Jesus quoted from this passage, "The Spirit of the Lord is on me, because he has anointed me to preach good news to the poor. He has sent me to proclaim freedom for the prisoners and recovery of sight for the blind, to release the oppressed, to proclaim the year of the Lord's favor" (Luke 4:18,19). Jesus came to bring restoration, to set the captives free. He came to bring healing to the whole man; to the spirit, the soul, and the body. He's our Healer, our Deliverer, our Savior, our Provider, our Protector.

"Instead of their shame my people will receive a double portion, and instead of disgrace they will rejoice in their inheritance; and so they will inherit a double portion in their land and everlasting joy will be theirs" (Isaiah 61:7). I have an inheritance in the Lord and everlasting joy; I have received so many good things from Him. And He has many more good things to give to me.

Surely goodness and mercy shall follow me all the days of my life; and I will dwell in the house of the Lord forever.

Psalm 23:6 reminds me of the love my Shepherd pours out on my life—God *so* loves me. I almost cannot comprehend such favor, but I want to. I want to rest in His leading, find comfort in His presence, and shout His praises in victory. I want to grow deeper in Him. It seems that for a long time in my walk with the Lord, I've been a sheep. But there comes a time when you have to be a shepherd also.

"Lord, you know all things; you know that I love you." Jesus said, "Feed my sheep."

JOHN 21:17

Shepherd of souls, refresh and bless
Thy chosen pilgrim flock
With manna in the wilderness,
With water from the rock.

We would not live by bread alone,
But by that word of grace,
In strength of which we travel on
To our abiding place.

JAMES MONTGOMERY

When people look at my paintings, I want them to see the beauty God uses in His creation. When people get through looking at my work, I want them to feel a little touch of satisfaction. When the world was created, Genesis says, "God saw all that he had made, and it was very good" (Genesis 1:31).

You are a work of art too. God is painting a wonderful picture on the canvas of your life. Sometimes He uses dark colors, but they are only there so that the light is even more beautifully contrasted. I believe God uses a lot of light in His work, and also weaves in images of still water and green pastures. I don't know yet where the end of my journey will be, but I do know this...I will follow after Him all the days of my life, and when this life is over, I will dwell in His house with Him forever. May you be there too.

He tends his flock like a shepherd; He gathers the lambs in his arms and carries them close to his heart . . .

ISAIAH 40:11